About
THE
LIZARD

To Fiona, David
with love

Sam, Paul

Dec 1991

BOSSINEY BOOKS

First published in 1989 by
Bossiney Books,
St Teath, Bodmin, Cornwall.

Printed and bound by
R Booth (Bookbinders) Ltd.,
Mabe Burnthouse, Cornwall.

Typeset by
Helston Printers Ltd.,
Cornwall

PLATE ACKNOWLEDGEMENTS
Front cover photography by
Roy Westlake

Back cover photography by Ray Bishop

Ray Bishop pages: 5, 8, 9, 21, 22, 24, 25,
29, 31, 37, 39, 42, 47, 49, 51, 53, 54, 57, 60,
61

Felicity Young pages: 7, 11, 41, 46, 48, 50,
52, 55, 56, 59, 62

Cornish Studies Library pages: 16, 17, 27,
28, 35.

The site of the original slipway for the Lizard lifeboat at Polpeor Cove. Nearby are boards recording the many services rendered by the Lizard lifeboat.

About the Author and the Book

A Cornishman, Michael Williams started full-time publishing in 1975. With his wife Sonia, he runs Bossiney Books from a cottage and converted barn in North Cornwall - they are literally cottage publishers, specialising in Westcountry subjects by Westcountry authors. For ten years, they ran the Bossiney House Hotel, just outside Tintagel - hence the name Bossiney Books.

In addition to publishing and writing, Michael Williams is a keen cricket enthusiast and collector of cricket books. He is President of the Cornish Crusaders Cricket Club and a member of the Cornwall and Gloucestershire County Clubs. He is also a member of the RSPCA, and has actively worked for reform in laws relating to animal welfare. In 1984, he was elected to the Ghost Club, and remains convinced Cornwall is the most haunted area in the whole of Great Britain.

His most recent publications are *St. Ives* and *Hawker's Morwenstow*. As a publisher in 1988 he launched his first Dorset titles, and Bossiney now covers five areas: Cornwall, Devon, Dorset, Somerset and Avon.

Here in *About The Lizard,* he explores a favourite area of Cornwall. 'For the purpose of this publication I'm concentrating on The Lizard itself, and just a few of the places on either side, starting at Kynance Cove and ending at Kennack Sands on the eastern flank.'

Michael Williams

About The Lizard

The Lizard is Britain's farthest south.

This is a unique corner of Cornwall: a region of contrasts, the cradle of the age of Wireless, the haunt of smugglers - the Earth Satellite Station on Goonhilly Downs and yet the peninsula of those courageous Saints.

Lizard is the heel of Cornwall; whereas Land's End is the toe, and Mount's Bay the sole. A magical place, where you can renew your batteries. You cannot 'do' the Lizard in a day or a week or a lifetime. It is a renewing, ongoing experience. For some people Lizard can be a new beginning - for others the end of the world, as indeed it was on many occasions, for this coastline is littered with wrecks - and echoes of the past.

Denys Val Baker, who sailed around our jagged Cornish coastline and wrote about it so well, once said of the Lizard: 'I'm never so relieved as when our boat has finally rounded that squat seemingly endless point, with all its dangerous off lying rocks...' Layers of history and legend cloak the land and the sea hereabouts, and sometimes it is difficult to know where one begins and the other ends.

Lizard has the ability to surprise us - make us think.

This mini tour begins at Kynance and ends at Kennack Sands. Come then let us explore this lovely, haunting place. Where better to begin? Kynance, where we shall be following Royal footsteps in the sand and across the rocks.

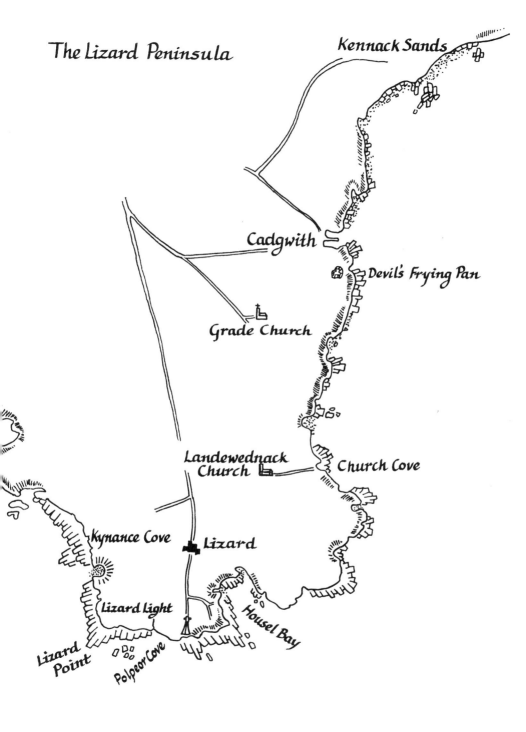

The Lizard Peninsula

Kennack Sands

Cadgwith

Devil's Frying Pan

Grade Church

Landewednack
Church

Church Cove

Kynance Cove

Lizard

Lizard Light

Housel Bay

Lizard
Point

Polpeor Cove

Kynance Cove

Somebody called Kynance 'One of the most beautiful coves in Cornwall.' But they were wrong. Kynance is simply one of the finest coves in all Britain. Moreover it has a timeless quality.

Murray's Guide, published back in 1859, said: 'The rocks appear as if they had been purposely grouped; and by their dark but varied colours pleasingly contrast with the light tints of the sandy beach and azure sea. The predominent colour of the serpentine is an olive green, but this is diversified by waving lines of red and purple, while many of the rocks are encrusted by the yellow lichen, or warmed by veins of steatite. The fragments into which the cliffs have been dissevered are pierced by caverns which are beautifully polished by the waves, and the beach is strewed with gorgeous pebbles.' And that is the essential spirit and character of Kynance today. Kynance is derived from the ancient Cornish language 'kenans', meaning enclosed valley.

Kynance: It was in 1846 that Prince Albert and the Royal children landed here, 'and by their kind condescension won for themselves golden opinions among the few of Her Majesty's loving Cornish subjects who chanced to be on the spot...'

Photographer Ray Bishop looks towards Lizard Town from the cliffs beyond and above Kynance Cove.

860. Kynance.

Caves are mysterious places - as this old picture postcard shows at Kynance. It was taken by Mr. Hawke of Helston, a well-known Cornish photographer in the heyday of postcard correspondence.

Kynance Cove

This photograph of Kynance was taken in the year 1895. Housed in The Cornish Studies Library at Redruth, it has a comprehensive caption which reads as follows:

'Here we have the most picturesque and striking scene in the Lizard promontory. It is useless to visit Kynance except at low water; it may easily be explored by ladies, but strangers are warned to pay strict attention to the state of the tide, for by lingering too long, beguiled by the varied attractions of the place, they risk having their retreat cut off by the rising water. A steep path through a notch or chine in the cliffs, here composed of dark serpentine, leads down to the shore at a spot cumbered with huge broken fragments, the remains of a cave which has fallen in. Scrambling over these, round a corner of rock generally washed by the tide, you enter a land-locked amphitheatre, or oval recess, deserted by the waves at low water from two to four hours every tide, leaving a broad expanse of white sand shut out from the sea by a group of lofty isolated rocks, rising in fantastic shapes of towers, pinnacles and obelisks. The biggest of these is called Asparagus Island, because that plant used to grow wild upon it.

On the land side this arena is walled in by lofty, overhanging cliffs, at whose base, are several wave-washed caverns, to which fanciful names have been given, such as the Kitchen Parlour, Drawing-room and so on. The most prominent object in the Cove is a narrow, pinnacled rock, known as the Steeple, which rises in the middle like a huge obelisk. Between it and Asparagus Island is a deep chasm, which at certain states of the tide exhibits a curious phenomenon. A narrow fissure, fancifully denominated the Devil's Bellows, pierces the island and runs from the sea to the cove.'

Lizard Magic

Lady Clara Vyvyan, who lived at Trelowarren for many years, was one of Cornwall's finest descriptive writers. She knew the Lizard intimately. No man or woman has written about Lizard Country with greater perception -or passion. She once said: 'If I were asked to describe the country briefly, I should use the single word *magic.*' In *My Cornwall*, first published by Bossiney in 1973, she reflected:

'It has that same magic which may be felt now and then in the work of great artists, whether it be enshrined in paint or words or marble that sense of 'something more' behind or beyond or beneath things tangible or visible. One may come across it suddenly, elusive but haunting, in certain lines of poetry.

'....Intermittently, in the course of a long life, I have often felt this same magic in certain aspects and qualities of the Lizard peninsula. To imprison those things in words is not an easy task and some of them are dangerously near extinction, threatened by the noise, ugliness and crowds of the industrial age.

Perhaps if we go back in time for more than half a century to a certain summer when I spent many days in that country, I can explain what its atmosphere of magic meant to me then and how it persists now, not only in memory but in actuality. For it was concerned with streams and their secret undergrowth and the coastal track that led along high cliffs and down into valleys, with bird life and wild flowers and moorland space; and these things have not yet been obliterated in this obliterating age of the bull-dozer.'

Lady Clara Vyvyan in her twenties.

Lizard Town

They may call it Lizard Town, but it is, in fact, no more than a village. Moreover even loyal locals will confess Lizard Town is not beautiful: a colony of buildings apparently constructed without much thought in terms of style or position. The superficial visitor may hurry away, but he is mistaken. The truth is this parish of Landewednack is full of history and legend - and unexpected beauty.

J. C. Trewin referred to The Lizard as 'a rumble of serpentine workers' huts,' and nowhere else on the whole peninsula is the craft more evident. In wooden sheds the craftsmen work away - sometimes as their fathers did before them. They turn the stone into lighthouses, paperweights, ashtrays - you can buy serpentine bracelets and cufflinks.

Tourism, of course, has changed the commercial character of Lizard like the rest of Cornwall. A visitor in the middle of the last century wrote: 'The collection of cottages which is dignified with the name of Lizard-town contains little worthy of note. The inhabitants are in general quiet, industrious, and orderly, gaining their livelihood by fishing, or working as day-labourers in the fields...' That nineteenth century visitor would, of course, find big changes today; yet the essential magic of the place remains -for those who are prepared to get out and about and that means getting beyond the centre of Lizard town.

This delightful thatched cottage above Church Cove is known as the Mariners. A three-storey cottage is a rarity in Cornwall. Once a kiddlywink or ale house, it was, for a while, the home of Jack Train, a member of Tommy Handley's *Itma* team in the heyday of 'the wireless'.

Church Cove on a peaceful day, photographed by Mr.
Hawke of Helston for a postcard.

All roads lead from Lizard Town.

Life looked more idyllic when this old photo of Church Cove was taken. Whether it was quite so comfortable when the winds howled under doors and through ill-fitting windows and doing the washing meant a trip to the well on a cold winter's day is questionable.

Examples of Serpentine craft on sale at the Regent Cafe and Gift Shop, Lizard Town.

Lizard, Old Cottages.

Well, who could resist a Cornish cream tea outside such a pretty cottage. This old picture postcard conjures up visions of eternal summer and even the notice above the front door offers boats for hire, wonder if they supplied a boatman too.

Church Cove, overleaf, has a private air - even today. Little wonder that this part of the Lizard coastline has such a reputation for smuggling and smugglers. Local folklore has it that when a 'run' was being made, a look-out was strategically placed on the church tower, enabling him to observe both the approach road and the seashore. Some Lizard people say a former rector neglected some of his spiritual duties because he was too busy with his other calling - that of 'free trader'. Cornish smuggling was at its particular high noon in the eighteenth century, when high taxes made it a lucrative business. One visiting writer penned: 'the coasts here swarm with smugglers from the Land's End to the Lizard....'

Motor buses brought visitors to the Lizard in the 1900s. Here is the scene outside Hill's Hotel at the Lizard, kept by Mr. James Hill. Originally a farmhouse flanked by fields, it later became The Lizard Hotel. Today it has a third name: The Top House. A pub, just down the road, virtually next door, once existed alongside and locals had the habit of saying: 'Well, now I'm going for a drink at the top house!'

The Lizard. Beacon Terrace.

A photograph of Beacon Terrace, the Lizard, taken around 1900. If any of these children are alive today, then they will be somewhere between the age of 90 and 100.

Painter and book illustrator Felicity Young looks out into the Channel on a windswept morning in winter. All Felicity's drawings inside these pages have been especially commissioned for this publication. On this, her first visit to the Lizard peninsula, she said: 'It's unlike anywhere else in the whole of Cornwall'.

Jean Stubbs and
100 Years Around The Lizard

One present day author who knows, understands and loves the Lizard peninsula is Jean Stubbs who lives at Nancegollan on the other side of Helston. The author of sixteen novels, many of her short stories have been televised and adapted for radio. It was in 1985 that Bossiney published her *100 Years Around the Lizard.* Touring the area, and aided by some wonderful old pictures, she turned the calendars back, transporting the reader on an incredible time machine. Not surprisingly the book immediately won golden opinions from resident and visitor alike.

In it Jean Stubbs delved into that fascinating subject of the very name.

'The Lizard's old name was *Meneage,* meaning 'a monastic land'. As S H Burton said "The Saints have set their seal on it." So where does its newer name come from? *Lazer,* the leper? There is a leper's window in Landewednack Church. A view from the sea when the promontory looks like a lizard sunning itself?

'No, *Lis-arth* means the high court or fortress. Aptly-named, for this southern-most point of the British Isles stands majestically above its guardian rocks. At once secretive and intimate, sunlit and brooding, it has a thousand changes of mood and light. For six months of the year modern transport makes it accessible to visitors. Once they are gone Old Lizard returns to solitude, a place in which to be quiet, a place in which to find oneself.'

For anyone wanting to explore the Lizard peninsula, then Jean

Novelist Jean Stubbs signing copies of her book *100 Years Around The Lizard,* at the Bossiney Literary Lunch.

Stubbs' *100 Years Around the Lizard* is an investment. Here is more than a journey back in mood and time, it is a real insight into the people and the place. A perceptive reviewer in *Cornish Life* reflected: '... the true flavour of life on the windswept peninsula, past and present... the strange qualities of the flat landscape, the effects of the elements on people's lives and, above all, the contrast of past and present are distilled....'

Group Captain Leonard Cheshire VC, DSO, DFC, a man who became a double legend in half a lifetime. In the Hitler war Leonard Cheshire became a legend in the air with Bomber Command and later with single-minded Christian missionary zeal on behalf of the chronic sick. His name today is known in many parts of the world. It was on the Lizard, at Predennack, that he opened one of his first Cheshire Homes.

Lizard and the Armada

J.C. Trewin contributed a splendid chapter to *Both Sides of Tamar*, an early Bossiney title and now long out of print, only to be found in second-hand bookshops scattered over Devon and Cornwall. In it he recalled his Lizard roots. A distinguished author and London theatre critic, Mr. Trewin wrote:

'At any season the place was full of characters: my First Witch, a perfectly harmless crone from mid-village, who seemed to spend her time wrecking, combing the beaches for driftwood or any of the flotsam - varying between corks, oranges, and fountain-pen fillers -the sea might throw up between Housel and Caerthillian; a muscular, swarthy man who had a Spanish name, pronounced as spelt, and a trick of carrying on any conversation at a range of two hundred yards; and a bearded postman, with a bullseye lantern, who liked to read aloud any postcards he delivered to you. This was a child's response. The lonely ingrowing village was a community of friends.

'For any child a splendid world. At heart, I am sure, it has not changed, though too much is happening on Goonhilly Downs, the dark barrens (the "wylde moore called Gunhilly"), that we first cross on the road from Helston. The huge naval airfield of Culdrose sprawls over the site of my grandfather's farm; elsewhere, an obtrusive radio contraption must baffle anyone who thinks yet in terms of Marconi at Mullion. Once we get to it, Lizard Town is much as it used to be, especially when the visitors and their cars have pulled out and the South can lapse again into its proper peace. The South...but we have also to recognise Compton MacKenzie's words: 'The magic of the West that haunts the air from Boscay to the Hesperides is no more potent than in the Meneage, where - as in the north-west the basalt - the serpentine breaks into the granite rock as strange as the Phoenician trafficker of long ago.'

'Looking back, I remember at random the churring of the serpentine -workers' wheels, lamplight on the polished stone, the faded brocade of clifftop turf, a smell of geranium, musk and seaweed, the tale of *Moyar Diu* read on Pentreath beach, the masts of the barque *Queen Margaret* canted over in wreck. Much more: Housel pools starred with anemones, those broad double hedges on which we walked to Kynance or Cadgwith - a stranger called it "trudging on a fence" - white-tissued sea-mists ("squitchery" weather), a lane behind the church where we gathered sloes, Landewednack rookery at evening, sunsets that flowered above The Rill, and the escalading darting rush of coastline from Old Lizard across to Kynance. The names are a litany: Pentreath, Caerthillian, Pistol, Poleor, Housel, Penolver, Kilcobben, Polbream.

'Once I had the joy of presenting prizes at the village school where I went for two years. On that summer day I was able to tell young Landewednack about my personal obsession: the Spanish Armada on the Lizard sea. It sailed up from the South on a July afternoon in 1588. Watchers high on The Rill saw it coming. They heard the mutter of cannon as the Lord High Admiral of Spain, Don Alonzo de Guzman, Duke of Medina-Sidonia, had a consecrated, gold-embroidered banner run to his masthead, and every galleon in his fleet, the squadrons of Portugal and Biscay, of Castile and Andalusia, Guypuscoa and the Levant, fired a broadside:

' "A dying fall, a fading wraith,
A sound soon hushed again,
The Great Armada's whispered breath,
The ghostly guns of Spain."

'Rapidly, warning beacons flared along the Cornish coast. Anyone who stood that evening on Penolver would have discerned the Armada far out, vague shapes, upon each sail a great red cross; the galleons moving slowly forward in an oblique crescent, seven miles from tip to tip, "like the moon when it lies upon its back," with all the chivalry of Spain on board: Don Alonzo de Leyva, Don Diego de Valdez, Don Juan Martinez de Recalde, Don Miguel de Oquendo, Don Martin de Bretandona.'

' "There," my father would say to me when he was at home: "There boy - that's where the Dons came up from southward." And, just as I would strain to see Brazil, so I would gaze hopefully from Penolver into the dazzle of the afternoon across an empty southern sea.'

A photograph from the year 1935 which typifies the Lizard and its long tradition of lifesaving. A Danzig tanker went on to rocks in thick fog but was saved and refloated.

Pistol Meadow

Pistol Meadow is a grim reminder: this is beautiful but wicked coastline. Back in the 1700s, a transport ship was wrecked off the Maenheere Rocks - with horrific loss of life - there were only two survivors. The victims are buried here beneath the Tamarisk bushes in mass graves.

J. C. Trewin once recalled: 'I can believe anything of this meadow especially after a December sunset. It was in December that I had an odd experience, about four o'clock on a calm, dull afternoon during the Armistice Autumn. In the narrows of the cliff path above Pistol, I heard someone coming, a brisk patter of feet and stood aside to let him pass. He was, as I remember, a shrivelled man in a nondescript blue guernsey, badly torn at the collar. He had a fuzz of wiry, greying hair. Nothing else was noticeable, but his eyes, deep black in the extreme pallor of his face. I said "Good afternoon." He brushed by me, without answering. A few seconds later, not more, I heard steps again, and there coming towards me, was without a doubt the same man, though manifestly he could not have doubled round in so short a time and on so awkward a path. I stopped, more perplexed than frightened, and again said "Good afternoon." Again there was no reply. And then a third time, I heard steps. Now nothing was in sight. I felt a quick stirring in the air, but no-one passed me. Fear came, and I tore home through the darkening day.'

Testimony to the bravery of the men who risk their lives to save others.

Left board:

RECORD OF THE SERVICES
RENDERED BY
THE LIZARD LIFE-BOAT
OF THE
ROYAL NATIONAL LIFE-BOAT INSTITUTION

Aug 10 Schooner HURRELL of Fowey saved vessel and 4
Mar 23 Schooner SELINA of Swansea saved 2
Mar 4 Barque FORMALHAUT of Greifswald saved 11
Nov 11 Tug towing Barque EINTRACHT of Greifswald landed one
Nov 1 Brig LUIGIA E ROSA landed effects of crew
Jan 15 Brig SCOTSCRAIG of Dundee saved vessel and 9
Aug 9 S.S. MOSEL of Bremen saved 27
Jan 29 S.S. SUFFOLK of London saved 24
Mar 15 Schooner GIPSY QUEEN of Padstow saved 5
Mar 10 Barque LADY DUFFERIN of Plymouth saved 17
Mar 4 Barque GUSTAV BITTER of Newcastle saved 3
Mar 26 S.S. BENDO of Liverpool stood by
Nov 29 S.S. LANDORE of Liverpool saved 10
Aug 6 Barque VORTIGERN of London stood by
Nov 24 Barque GLIMT of Stavanger saved 4
Jan 17&18 S.S. SUEVIC of Liverpool (in six trips) saved 167
Mar 23 Ketch FANNY of Bideford saved 3
Feb 19 S.S. FLESWICK rendered assistance
    Lifeboat MINNIE MOON of Cadgwith gave help
Mar 3 Ship HANSY of Fredrikstad saved
Feb 15 Barque CHILI of Dunkirk helped to save vessel &20
Nov 5 Barque QUEEN MARGARET of Glasgow saved 27
Feb 23 Ship CROMDALE of Aberdeen saved 5
Mar 22 S.S. CORVUS of Swansea saved 9
Dec 31 Schooner FLORENCE of Fowey stood by
Jan 1920 S.S. ELWICK of Newcastle (H.M.Transport) landed 4
    do (second service) escorted to Newhaven
Mar 3 H.M.Drifter GLOAMING saved 15
Feb 13 S.S. DÉPUTÉ HENRY DURRE of Havre stood by
Jan 21 S.S. SAINT PATRICE of Havre landed twenty-three
Feb 10 Five-masted Schooner ADOLF VINNEN of Hamburg stood by
Feb 10 S.S. NIVELLE of London saved 20
Mar 3 S.S. BARDIC of Liverpool saved 93
    do second service rendered assistance
    8 do landed salvage party of thirty-seven
May 27 S.S. MAURICE BERNARD stood by
Feb 6 Ketch Barge LADY DAPHNE of Rochester saved 2
Feb 11 S.S. RUNNELSTONE of London stood by
Feb 27 Steam Trawler LE VIEUX TIGRE of Boulogne saved 18
Feb 20 Motor Tanker D.L.HARPER of Danzig saved 5
    21 do stood by and saved 38
Mar 26 S.S. CLAN MALCOLM of Glasgow stood by
Mar 8 S.S. RUBAAN of Glasgow saved 8
Feb 24 German aircraft landed body and saved 1
Feb 6 H.M.S. ML115 assisted to save vessel
Mar 12 M.V. MARGURETTE MARIE LOUISE of Belgium
    towed vessel to Newlyn
Feb 27 Torpedoed Steamship landed body
Apr 21 S.S. JOHN R.PARK of San Francisco stood by
Feb 2 M.V. KRONSBERG Hamburg stood by

Right board:

RECORD OF THE SERVICES
AND BOAT RECORD OF
THE LIZARD LIFE-BOATS
OF THE
ROYAL NATIONAL LIFE-BOAT INSTITUTION

SERVICES (continued)

1952 Jan 10 S.S. FLYING ENTERPRISE of New York stood...
1954 Jul 4 Naval Sailing Whaler salved whaler
    Jul 6 Firefly Aircraft salved wreckage
1955 Mar 31 Avenger Aircraft saved
    Jun 26 Yacht ENCHANTRESS of St Ives saved abandoned
1956 Jan 2 M.V. CITRINE of Glasgow saved
    Mar 2 Steam Tug CRUISER of Glasgow gave help
    M.V. CRETE AVON of London stood by & gave
    Jul 20 R.N.A.S. Aircraft assisted to locate wrecked aircraft
    Aug 20 Raft L'EGARÉ landed one
    (Second service) do towed to Falmouth
1957 Mar 25 M.V. CORALLO of Trieste escorted to Falmouth
    Aug 2 Motor Boat PINDA of Mullion saved boat and
1959 Jul 3 Yacht DREAM saved yacht and
1960 Aug 2 Naval Whaler towed whaler and 5 to Porthleven
1961 Jan 30 Sloop Yacht BULLFROG saved yacht and

BOAT RECORD

1859	1866	1st ANNA MARIA	Rescues
1866	1873	2nd ANNA MARIA	"
1873~1885		3rd ANNA MARIA	"
1885~1903		EDMUND & FANNY	"
1903~1918		ADMIRAL Sir GEORGE BACK	" 23
1918~1919		Sir FITZROY CLAYTON	"
1920~1934		FREDERICK H.PILLEY	" 13
1934~1961		DUKE OF YORK	"

When returning to Station after routine exercise on 7 Jan 18.. the first of the Lizard lifeboats capsized and was broken up on the rock below sadly three of the six men aboard were drowned.
— Coxswain Peter Mitchell —
Second Coxswain Richard Harris : Crewman Nicholas Stephen..

From this point on the night of the 17 March 1907 and throughout the morning of the following day, was witnessed the greatest ever rescue operation undertaken by lifeboats of the Royal National Lifeboat Institution when the White Star liner SUEVIC stranded on the Maenheere Reef in thick fog and heavy seas. In all, four lifeboats were involved in the rescue, those of the Lizard, Cadgwith, Coverack and Porthleven. In all 524 persons aboard the liner of whom 164 were women & children were saved. The Lizard lifeboat accounted for 167.

In 1961 this station was closed, the boathouse is no longer the responsibility of the R.N.L.I. The Lizard lifeboat which now alone serves the area is situated in Kilcobben Cove - 1 mile East of Polpeor..

Lower plaque:

The Royal National Lifeboat Institution is a charity whose sole purpose is saving life at sea. Its only source of income is by way of public donation and subscription. Lifeboatmen are volunteers who are prepared to put to sea at any time, in any weather to help those in peril.
Seventy-six pence of every pound donated to the R.N.L.I. goes towards providing lifeboatmen with the very best lifeboats and equipment available. We need your help to provide this back-up that they surely deserve.

Lizard Lights

The great Cornish historian A K Hamilton Jenkin, who lived inland at Redruth, told the tale of the old sailor who, departing this life, asked the parson to read the passage from the Scriptures, 'where they do tell about the Lezar' Lights'. Fortunately the cleric remembering verses from Genesis of the 'lesser Lights' which ruled the night, was able to tell the old man the story of their creation.

In the days before radar, this piece of coastline was a notorious graveyard for numerous vessels. Yet locals violently opposed the positioning of a lighthouse here in the seventeenth century. The Cornish folk of those times complained that such a light would rob them of 'God's Grace' - their description of the substantial 'harvest' they reaped from shipwrecks.

Nevertheless the Lizard has the distinction of being Cornwall's senior sea light.

The man with the idea was Sir John Killigrew, whose family were notorious smugglers. He wanted a light for financial reasons - that he might charge dues to every vessel which sailed by in safety. The debate - for and against a lighthouse - rumbled on for years. Eventually in December 1619 a light burned here, but Killigrew ran into problems: opposition to the light persisted and he had great difficulty in collecting dues. Killigrew abandoned the light and returned to his former way of life - a more profitable one.

Not until, 1752 was another light erected on The Lizard, a brace of coal-fired lights providing the illumination. Lights and buildings were modernised in 1812 and then electrified in 1878.

There is a delightful story concerning one sleepy keeper who was employed at The Lizard during the Napoleonic wars. Slumbering at his post he had allowed the light to burn dangerously low. The captain of a passing government packet was so angry that he ordered

Lizard Light and Foghorn

his gunner to fire cannon shot at the 'wished' light. No damage: but in our imagination we can picture the startled activity of one rudely awakened keeper as he feverishly worked to stoke up the dying fire.

The lighthouse, an impressive building, is open to visitors most weekdays.

Lizard lighthouse has come a long way since that pair of coal-fired lights provided the warning illumination. At night its flashing white patterns - some four million candle power - can be seen 29 miles out to sea. With the aid of a computer, it now controls all the rock lighthouses in the South West - and will eventually become the only manned light in the region.

Lizard Lighthouse, drawn by Felicity Young: destined to become the only manned lighthouse in the whole of the South West.

Lizard seamen have a long and heroic tradition in the lifeboat service. Today two Lizard lifeboat stations have combined under the name of the Cadgwith-Lizard Lifeboat. It operates from Kilcobben Cove and Ray Bishop took this photograph on a cold December morning.

Housel Bay

This bay has an excellent bathing beach and is but ten minutes walk from Lizard Town. Periodically scoured by storms, the beach always returns in due course. Above the beach stands the Housel Bay Hotel which rightly claims to be the 'most southerly hotel' in the kingdom. Over the years, the hotel has had some eminent guests, including royalty: Prince George, later King George V stayed here. C L Dodgson, who wrote under the nom de plume of Lewis Carroll stayed at Housel too. Did the author of *Alice in Wonderland* find some creative inspiration here? It is a very likely thought, for this whole coastline fans the imagination.

Daws Hugo

Nearby is a great hole shaped by a collapsed cave. It has alternative names: Daws Ogo or Daw Hugo - Ogo is an old Cornish word for cave. C A Johns, the enterprising cleric, who wrote *A Week at the Lizard* came here 140 years ago:

'After the spring tides in the beginning of July I visited it again for the purpose of ascertaining its depth, which, I found, had increased, and the floor was no longer level, but shelved towards the sea. On letting down a plummet-line I found that the weight would not rest at a depth of sixty feet, and suspecting what had taken place I descended the face of the cliff with the object of exploring the Daws' Hugo. The entrance to this cave, which can only be reached at low water, is about eight feet wide, and I should suppose about thirty feet high, divided half way up by a horizontal layer of rocks. As I approached I saw light streaming in from the extremity of the cave, which could only proceed from the bottom of the pit; a large quantity of rubbish was still left, but it was evident that this would in time be washed away, and that eventually the sea will enter the pit through the cave at high water, where in stormy weather, it will bear no fanciful resemblance to a huge boiling cauldron....'

Daw's Hugo

Landewednack Church

'The church (St Winwallo) is among elms and sycamores on a sheltered slope with old colour-washed cottages near, a change from the Lizard village above.' That was how Sir John Betjeman, the Poet Laureate, remembered the place when he came in the early 1960s.

Here in Landewednack Church, the most southerly church in all Britain, the last service in Cornish was preached: the year was 1678. The present day pulpit is made of polished chunks of serpentine, that stone which somehow symbolizes Lizard, setting it apart from the rest of Cornwall.

Out in Landewednack Churchyard, think of brave Robert Sampson, rector in the 1640s, when the plague struck. Truly a man of God, he continued to work among his people in a nightmare experience, administering the last rites, and comforting those who mourned. Inevitably he caught the plague, and lies buried with many of his people by these Cornish elms.

This parish also produced a sturdy cleric in the person of Thomas Cole who is reputed to have walked to Penryn and back, a distance of roughly twenty five miles, at the incredible age of 120, surely worth a place in *The Guinness Book of Records.*

As you go away take with you some words by another rector of Landewedack, G. Frederick Simpson:

> *'Pause, stranger, as you pass beneath*
> *Where Norman art and Gothic skill*
> *Have wrought a miracle in stone*
> *That time has made more lovely still*
> *Here, in this shrine, above this sea,*
> *There breathes the faith that made you free.'*

Beautiful words, but then this is a beautiful place.

Landewednack Church, overleaf, dedicated to Saint Winwallo, boasts a splendid tower: contrasting blocks of pinkish granite and dark green serpentine. There is something deeply appealing about this ancient shrine. There is a sense of Cornish history too in that the bells of Landewednack have been ringing out for some six centuries.

Headstone with sculptured gull in Landewednack Church-yard.

Felicity Young.

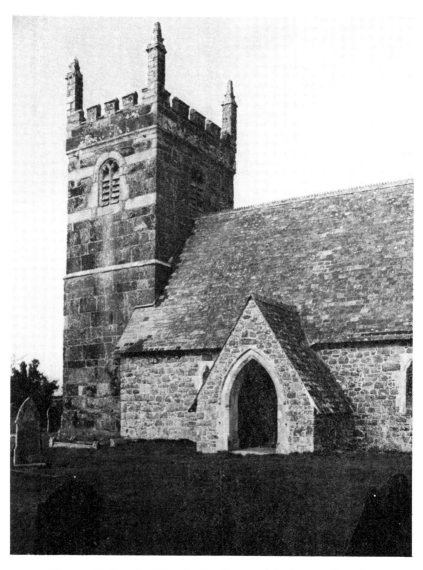

The small church of Grade stands surprisingly remote and high on the landscape of Lizard - its fourteenth century tower looking across green fields to the sea. It provokes a certain curiosity: 'Why here?'

Grade Church stands inland from Cadgwith. Felicity
Young's drawing shows the lovely stone work which went
into the building of this remote Lizard church.

Cadgwith

'One of Cornwall's lesser-known coves....'

That was the verdict of a certain travel writer
within the last twenty years. It is hard to imagine a more wildly
inaccurate statement. The truth is Cadgwith is almost too pretty to
be true. In a sentence, Cadgwith must be nearly everybody's idea -
and ideal - of a Cornish fishing cove. On a good summer's day it has
the air of the Mediterranean.

Whether you come in a car or on a cycle or on foot, you drop
down into Cadgwith, white-washed cottages clinging to the steep
narrow roadway and clustered around the beach where fishing boats
are winched up above high tide mark. You will find holiday
accommodation and, for the coastal path walker, a welcome inn, but
Cadgwith is still a working place in that fishermen earn their living

Cottages at Cadgwith

Devil's Frying Pan

here by catching crab and lobster. The two tiny beaches are divided by 'The Todden' a diminutive headland.

There is no harbour and the local boats launch and retrieve from the slipway in the old style. Between the years 1859 and 1955, Cadgwith had its lifeboat and during that period of time the Cadgwith lifeboat saved as many as 552 lives: a then Cornish record.

A number of buildings are thatched, a relatively unusual sight in Cornwall where slate has dominated since the nineteenth century -some of the eaves are chained down.

Motorists are strongly advised to use the car park up the valley. One tourist, Walter White of London, back in 1854 needed no such advice. In high summer he struggled, on foot, along the cliffs to Lizard in a gale - which almost drove him headlong into a chasm nearby. The Devil's Frying Pan is a considerable crater, where the roof of a deep cave has fallen in, leaving an arch of rock with boiling seas below. Little wonder that Walter White said Cornwall appeared 'to be subjected to visitations from the Evil One.' Like Wilkie Collins, he found this area of Cornwall charged with Supernatural undertones. Daphne du Maurier has said 'The time to walk about the Lizard headland is in winter or early spring... ' Then the sense of the past is often strongest.

Cadgwith on a Saturday morning out of season.

Lizard seamen have a long and heroic tradition in the lifeboat service. Today two Lizard lifeboat stations have combined under the name of the Cadgwith-Lizard lifeboat. It operates from Kilcobben Cove and Ray Bishop took this photograph on a cold December morning.

Thatched cottages at Cadgwith.

Boats at Cadgwith

Kennack Sands

Many people, who know their Cornwall, would rate Kennack Sands a favourite.

Here on the Lizard's eastern coast we come to the end of our mini-tour. Generations - locals and visitors alike - have enjoyed these twin sandy beaches: swimmers and surfers, sunbathers and children with their buckets and spades, all can find this a wonderful blend of sea and sand.

Our celebrated Cornwall-based novelist Dame Daphne du Maurier has happy childhood memories of Kennack Sands where she taught herself to swim. 'But to me, even then, the sea seemed

Author Michael Williams and artist Felicity Young enjoy a bracing walk across Kennack Sands on a wintry December morning.

cruel, demanding victims.' The grandmother of Captain Mark Phillips has long had a cottage hereabouts. It is a haunt too of geologists - there are four different rock types all within a few yards of each other - while the wheeling sea birds often provide their own bit of natural theatre. It is a magical place, somehow symbolizing the best qualities of the peninsula.

Yet curiously Kennack Sands remain strangely unwritten, almost ignored - either unmentioned by travel writers or dismissed in a few superficial lines. Interesting therefore that the Rev C A Johns on his Lizard exploration back in the 1840s gave his readers a detailed word picture:

'... a narrow yellow line idicates a sandy beach, known by the name of Kennack Sands. The opposite boundary of the bay is formed by a bold, bluff, head-land, the Black-head, a most appropriate name, for the whole face of the cliff, with the exception of one narrow perpendicular strip, called Sparnick, is of a remarkable dingy hue. In the distance, the Deadman Point is distinctly visible, with a vessel or two entering or quitting Falmouth Harbour, which lies between; and if the weather be very clear, the Rame Head the most easterly head-land in the country, may be described stretching out a long way on the horizon, as unsubstantial in appearance as a fog-bank. One or two lobster catchers are creeping along under the cliffs in their tiny vessels, and few fishing boats of a larger size are making for the offing, there to set their drift-nets, as soon as night sets in; just beneath us, on a projecting ledge of rock, lie the whitening bones of a lamb, killed and devoured by ravens, before it was strong enough to seek safety by flight; and the deep croak of the same bird, or the shrill note of the jackdaw, divides with the dashing of the sea below us and its murmuring roll beyond the whole empire of sound.'

Illustrator Felicity Young and photographer Ray Bishop, on a first time visit for these illustrations, came on an autumn morning and both thought it a 'tonic'.

That one word is perhaps the secret.

Provided we come in a receptive frame of mind, and with a proper degree of humility, Kennack Sands can speak to us, and we go on our way refreshed and renewed.

Rocks at Kennack Sands

Kennack Sands, above, captured by Cornish artist Felicity Young and on the previous pages by the camera of Ray Bishop.

Acknowledgements

A conversation with old friends at The Regent, out on the Lizard, in the late summer of 1988 revealed the need for a new title on the Lizard. We all agreed Jean Stubbs' *100 Years Around The Lizard* remains *the* book for the peninsula, but my friends reasoned: 'We need something smaller relating specifically to The Lizard itself and some of the coastline on either side.' This publication is the result.

I am once more indebted to The Cornish Studies Library at Redruth who have provided some of the old photographs - and helped me to unearth material from the past. Special thanks too, to Bossiney editor Alison Poole who spent a pleasant and profitable morning with me at Redruth delving into Lizard in the old days - and for her thoughful perceptive editing of this and other recent Bossiney titles. Linda Turner has typed the manuscript; Felicity Young has provided all the drawings - all especially shaped for *About The Lizard* - and Ray Bishop has done the modern photography. This then is essentially a team effort.

ALSO AVAILABLE

100 YEARS AROUND THE LIZARD
by Jean Stubbs
A beautiful title, relating to a magical region of Cornwall, well illustrated, with text by the distinguished novelist living near Helston.
'... brings a fresh insight... She writes with the skills of a professional novelist, the knowledge which comes from living here, and the enthusiasm which an inquiring mind can develop. She unfolds the layers of memory with a delightful selection of old photographs ...'
Douglas Williams, The Western Morning News

GREAT HOUSES OF CORNWALL
by Jean Stubbs
'... explores seven National Trust properties, digging deeply into the history of the contrasting area of Cornwall.'
John Marquis, The Packet Group of Newspapers

MY CORNWALL
A personal vision of this Celtic land by Daphne du Maurier, Ronald Duncan, James Turner, Angela du Maurier, Jack Clemo, Denys Val Baker, Colin Wilson, C.C. Vyvyan, Arthur Caddick, Michael Williams and Derek Tangye.
'... an ambitious collection of chapters.'
The Times, London

FESTIVALS OF CORNWALL
by Douglas Williams
Explores some of the great Cornish occasions in the calendar.
'Douglas Williams has come up trumps again ... captures the individual character of the county's festivals through his love of the Cornish and all things Cornish.'
The Cornishman

SUPERNATURAL ADVENTURE
by Michael Williams
Contains a great deal of unpublished material relating to the Supernatural.
'Spiritual healing, automatic writing are just a few of the spectrum of subjects ... neat, well-presented ... easy-to-read volume.'
Psychic News

SAINTS OF THE SOUTH WEST
by James Mildren
James Mildren describes 'Saints of the South West' as 'an adventure into the remote past of Cornwall and Devon ...' Moreover he believes 'The Saints still have a message for us all ...'

OTHER BOSSINEY TITLES INCLUDE

LEGENDS OF CORNWALL
Sally Jones

GHOSTS OF CORNWALL
Peter Underwood

MYSTERIOUS PLACES
Peter Underwood

SUPERNATURAL IN CORNWALL
Michael Williams

SEA STORIES OF CORNWALL
Ken Duxbury

COASTLINE OF CORNWALL
Ken Duxbury

E.V. THOMPSON'S WESTCOUNTRY

AROUND & ABOUT THE ROSELAND
David Mudd

THE CRUEL SEA
David Mudd

DISCOVERING BODMIN MOOR
E.V. Thompson